Our Amazing Solar System

MERCURY

Kerri Mazzarella

A Stingray Book

SEAHORSE PUBLISHING

Teaching Tips for Caregivers:

This Hi-Lo book features high-interest subject matter that will appeal to all readers in intermediate and middle school grades. It may be enjoyed by students reading at or above grade level as well as by those who are looking for age-appropriate themes matched with a less challenging reading level. Hi-Lo books are ideal for ELL readers, too.

Each book appeals to a striving reader's age and maturity level. Opportunities are provided for students to read words they already know while encountering a limited number of new, high-interest vocabulary words. With these supports in place, students will read more fluently while increasing reading comprehension. Use the following suggestions to help students grow as readers.

- Encourage the student to read independently at home.
- Encourage the student to practice reading aloud.
- Encourage activities that require reading.
- Establish a regular reading time.
- Have the student write questions about what they read.

Teaching Tips for Teachers:

Research shows that one of the best ways for students to learn a new topic is to read about it.

Before Reading

- Ask, "What do I know about this topic?"
- Ask, "What do I want to learn about this topic?"

During Reading

- Ask, "What is the author trying to teach me?"
- Ask, "How is this like something I already know?"

After Reading

- Discuss how the text features (headings, index, etc.) help with understanding the topic.
- Ask, "What interesting or fun fact did you learn?"

Table of Contents

Tiniest Planet 4

Now You See Me 6

Solid Surface 8

No Life Here 10

Hole-y Moly! 12

Spin, Baby, Spin 14

Moons or Rings? 16

Icy Hot 18

Always Learning 20

Glossary 22

Index 23

After Reading Questions 23

About the Author 24

Tiniest Planet

Mercury is the closest **planet** to the Sun in our **solar system**.

It is located about 36 million miles (58 million kilometers) from the Sun.

Mercury is also the smallest planet in our solar system.

It is only a little larger than Earth's moon.

Sun

Earth's moon

Mercury

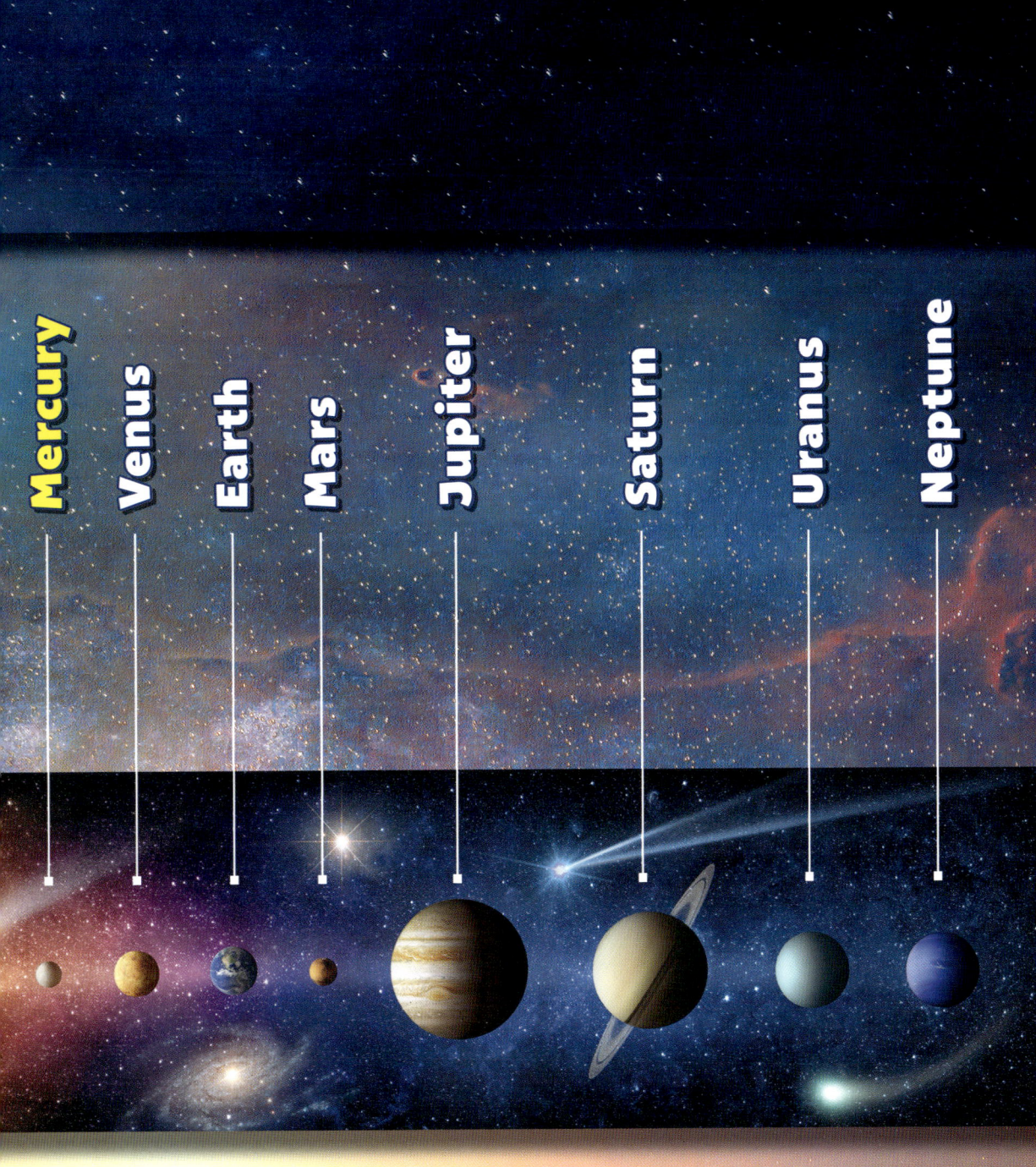

Mercury is one-third the width of Earth. You could fit 18 Mercuries inside Earth.

Now You See Me

Mercury is one of five planets that can be seen without a **telescope**.

Venus, Mars, Jupiter, and Saturn can also be seen with the naked eye.

Astronomers named Mercury after the fastest Roman god.

The name fits because Mercury moves so swiftly around the Sun.

The star we call the Sun would appear three times larger from the surface of Mercury than it does from Earth.

Solid Surface

Mercury, Venus, Earth, and Mars are the innermost planets in our solar system.

They are closest to the Sun.

Together, they are called **terrestrial** planets.

Like the others, Mercury has a solid, rocky surface.

Mars

Earth

Venus

Mercury

No Life Here

Mercury has an extremely thin **atmosphere**.

It is made up of hydrogen, helium, sodium, oxygen, and potassium.

There is little protection from the Sun's heat and from open space.

The extreme conditions make it impossible for life as we know it to exist on this planet.

Hole-y Moly!

Mercury's surface is covered in **craters**. Over 760 craters have been observed by scientists.

The thin atmosphere means that the planet is often hit by asteroids and comets. The crashes create craters.

Caloris Basin is the largest crater on Mercury. It is 960 miles (1,550 kilometers) wide.

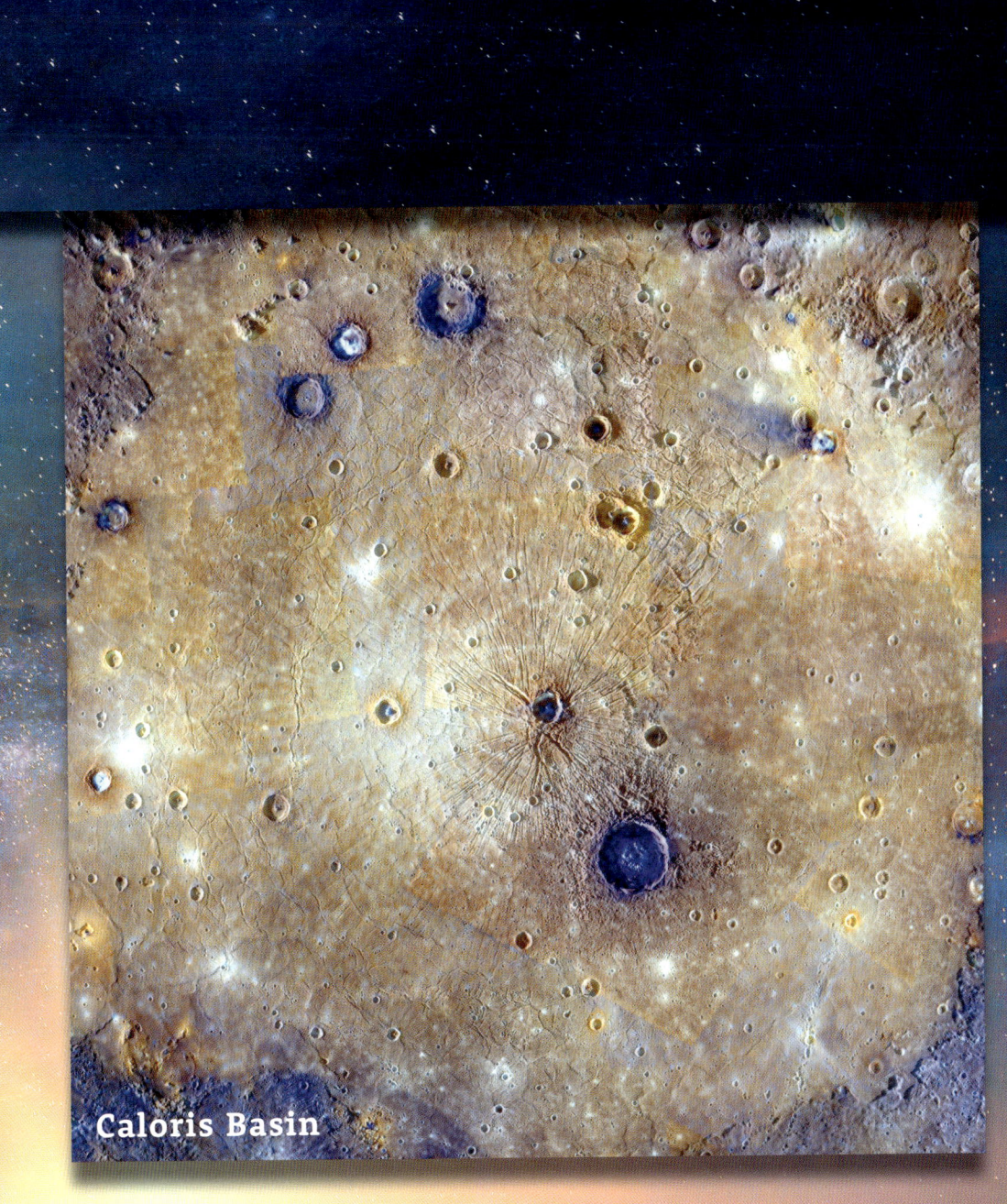

Caloris Basin

Asteroids and comets are small rocky objects that travel around the Sun.

Spin, Baby, Spin

Mercury has a short **orbit**. It takes just 88 Earth days for it to go once around the Sun.

Mercury travels through space at 29 miles (47 kilometers) per second. That's faster than any other planet in the solar system.

As it orbits the Sun, Mercury spins slowly on its **axis**. It takes 59 Earth days to make a full rotation.

Mercury's axis has almost no tilt. Because it spins upright, it has no seasons.

It takes a long time for the Sun to rise and set on Mercury. One full solar day, with a day and a night, takes 176 Earth days, or two years on Mercury.

Moons or Rings?

Some planets have several moons and impressive ring systems. But not Mercury.

It has no rings.

Mercury and Venus are the only planets in the solar system with zero moons. Yup, none!

Venus

Mercury

Earth's moon

Icy Hot

Mercury has the most extreme temperature changes of any planet in the solar system.

It averages 354 degrees Fahrenheit (179 degrees Celsius). But it can reach up to 800 degrees Fahrenheit (427 degrees Celsius) when facing the Sun. Only Venus is hotter.

When facing away from the Sun, the temperature can drop as low as –290 degrees Fahrenheit (–179 degrees Celsius).

In 1991, scientists discovered ice on Mercury's surface.

Always Learning

Scientists have gained valuable information by sending **spacecrafts** to Mercury.

Mariner 10 was the first to visit the planet in 1974. It took pictures of Mercury's surface.

Scientists around the world continue to learn new things about the closest planet to the Sun.

BepiColombo

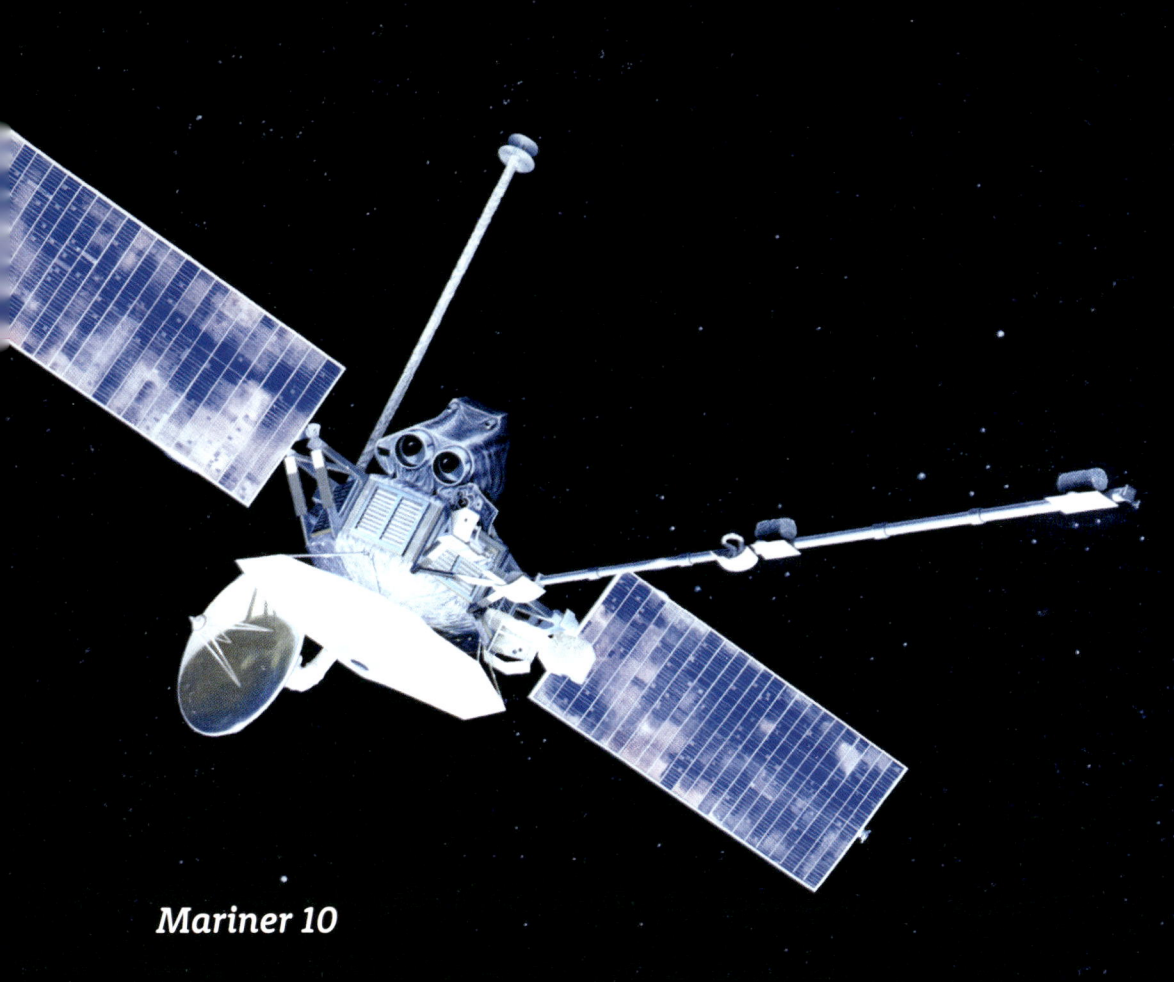

Mariner 10

BepiColombo was launched in 2018. It is scheduled to enter Mercury's orbit in 2025.

Glossary

astronomers (uh-STRAH-nuh-mers): people who study stars, planets, and space

atmosphere (AT-muhs-feer): the mixture of gases that surrounds a planet; all the air between the surface of a planet and outer space

axis (AK-sis): an imaginary line through the middle of an object, around which that object spins

craters (KRAY-turz): large holes in the ground caused by the impact of something falling or exploding, such as a meteorite crashing or a volcano erupting

orbit (OR-bit): the curved path followed by a moon, planet, or satellite as it circles a planet or a star like our Sun

planet (PLAN-it): a large heavenly body that orbits a star; Earth is a planet orbiting the star that we call the Sun

solar system (SOH-lur SIS-tuhm): the gravity-bound system of the star we call the Sun and the objects that orbit it, including eight planets; there are many solar systems in the universe

spacecrafts (SPAYS-krafts): vehicles that travel in space or that are used in space

telescope (TEL-uh-skope): an instrument that makes distant objects seem larger and closer; used especially for studying the stars and other heavenly bodies

terrestrial (tuh-RES-tree-uhl): made up of rocks or metals and having a hard surface

Index

asteroids 12, 13

BepiColombo 20, 21

day(s) 14, 15

ice 19

life 10

smallest 4

surface 7, 8, 12, 19, 20

temperature 18

After Reading Questions

1. Is life likely to exist on Mercury? Why or why not?

2. Describe the surface of Mercury.

3. Mercury is closest to the Sun. Is it the hottest planet in the solar system? How does Mercury's atmosphere help explain your answer?

About the Author

Kerri Mazzarella lives in south Florida with her husband, four children, and two dogs. She loves looking up at the night sky at all the stars! She lives near the Kennedy Space Center and likes to visit. Kerri enjoys learning all about planets and our solar system.

Written by: Kerri Mazzarella
Design by: Jen Bowers
Editor: Kim Thompson

Library of Congress PCN Data
Mercury / Kerri Mazzarella
Our Amazing Solar System
ISBN 978-1-6389-7976-0 (hard cover)
ISBN 979-8-8873-5035-6 (paperback)
ISBN 979-8-8873-5094-3 (EPUB)
ISBN 979-8-8873-5153-7 (eBook)
Library of Congress Control Number: 2022942007

Printed in the United States of America.

Photographs/Shutterstock: cover, p. 1, 4, 9, 16 Mercury © Vector Tradition; cover, p.1, 5, solar system ©2021 Triff; cover and interior background ©2020 Nuttawut Uttamaharad; cover, p.1, 9, 16 Venus © Vector Tradition; p.6 ©2020 Alexander_Safonov; p.7 ©2011 Mopic; p.8 ©2017 Nostalgia for Infinity; p.9 Earth and Mars Venus © Vector Tradition; p.10 ©2021 buradaki; p.11 ©2021 david.costa.art; p.12 Public Domain/NASA/Johns Hopkins University/APL; p.14 Public Domain/NASA/Johns Hopkins University/APL/Carnegie Institution of Washington; p.15 ©2017 Maxal Tamor; p.17 ©2017 kdshutterman; p.19 ©2017 alima007; p.20, 21 Public Domain/NASA/JPL

Seahorse Publishing Company

www.seahorsepub.com

Copyright © 2023 **SEAHORSE PUBLISHING COMPANY**

All rights reserved. No part of this publication may be reproduced, stored in a retrieval system or be transmitted in any form or by any means, electronic, mechanical, photocopying, recording, or otherwise, without the prior written permission of Seahorse Publishing Company.

Published in the United States
Seahorse Publishing
PO Box 771325
Coral Springs, FL 33077